Ann Sheridan

AS

Plate 1

Do not
cut out area
between arm
and body.

Do not
cut out area
between arm
and body.

AS

AS

Plate 2

Rita Hayworth

RH

Plate 3

Do not
cut out areas
between arms
and body.

Do not
cut out areas
between arms
and body.

RH

RH

Plate 4

Hedy Lamarr

HL

Plate 5

HL

Plate 6

Lana Turner

LT

Plate 7

LT

Plate 8

Dorothy Lamour

DL

Plate 9

DL

DL

Plate 10

Veronica Lake

VL

Plate 11

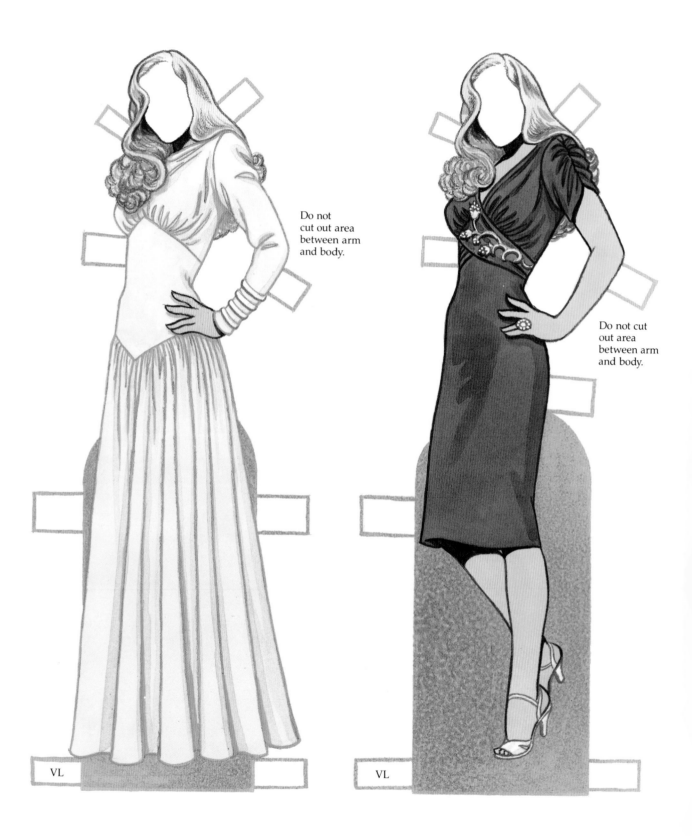

Do not
cut out area
between arm
and body.

Do not cut
out area
between arm
and body.

VL

VL

Plate 12

Gene Tierney

Plate 13

GT

GT

Plate 14

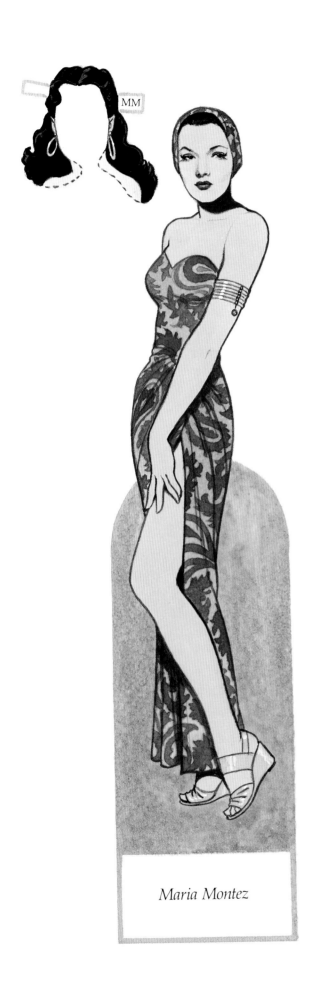

Maria Montez

Plate 15

MM

MM

Plate 16